The War Of Wall Street

Ashwin Krishna Kumar

ISBN: 1480203793
ISBN-13: 978-1480203792

For the people who do not get the credit they deserve for their work.

"Be the change you want to see in the world"

-Mahatma Gandhi

CONTENTS

Disclaimer

I am by no means elitist. I am by no means a rich spoiled kid who cares about nothing else. While this book may upset people (for which I profusely apologize), that is not my hope. My hope is to have people educated about who we are to blame for the recent financial crisis. It is my hope that as a nation we can coexist harmoniously with Wall Street and respect what they do. Once again I apologize for anything you may deem to be excessive, I am only calling it like I see it.

INTRODUCTION

<u>The War of Wall Street</u> entails how each demographic in society perceive and interact with Wall Street. Dealing with the fallout from the 2008 financial crisis has led many people to wrongly point fingers at the major banks while using questionable logic and evidence. To further illustrate this phenomena let me explicate on a personal anecdote. When I was young I had an extreme dislike for trying new foods- and still do to a lesser extent. And when something new would be pushed into my face, I would immediately respond by getting up from the table and leaving. Eventually, this got out of hand. My parents then decided that in order to dictate that I disliked something I had to taste it. If, I didn't taste the new dish my toys would get taken away. Anyway, the point to the story is peoples' experiences with Wall Street are akin to my food situation.

People place hate where it can easily be placed. And let's face it the rich bankers are the easiest place to point. The reason this exists is:

1. Misguided hate
2. Lack of knowledge about the history of Wall Street
3. Lack of knowledge about role of Wall Street

But I believe in order to dislike something a hint of knowledge of that subject is warranted. Anyway, the origins of Wall Street have been disputed but many suggest that the name derives from a Dutch wall in pre-colonial New York. Skip to the year 1776 when a country is born. At that time in the Empire State at the intersection of Broad Street and Wall Street was a buttonwood tree that was the gathering place for the investors and traders. In 1817, all the traders and investors decided to make a group known today as the New York Stock Exchange. The turn of the 19th century was not what Wall Street looks like today with both business and housing dominating the landscape until the opening of the Erie Canal. The land became increasingly enticing to banks who could HELP people selling their goods and thus expand businesses. Wall Street really took off during the Civil War when financing for the economic boom became a necessity. People then turned to banks in order to grow their business during the harsh times. The war also allowed one of the most influential bankers to build his empire. A man from Hartford, Connecticut -whose name may appear on your credit card statement every month- John Pierpont (J.P.) Morgan. His rise brought Wall Street to a new level of fame. Morgan was also instrumental in bringing other "Empire builders" such as Charles Dow to Wall Street, who then with the likes of Morgan led a successful wave of industry that has yet to be matched. The 20th century led to the formation of companies that make up the historic, rustic, yet bustling Wall Street of today. The history of these firms has been tainted by the likes of the Great Depression as well as the recent depression. However, the overall of ideology of Wall Street has remained firm, with its sole purpose of creating capital and expanding business. Yet I feel there are a couple of fundamental aspects of Wall Street that we as Americans forget:

1 The importance of Wall Street
2 Why 90% of the population is wrong

Wall Street is important in an abundant number of ways. Other than being the driving force for the United States economy, Wall Street accounts for almost 40% of New York City's taxable income as well as accounting for 9% of the city's employment rate. Despite the size of New York the money is still a lot. What this means for all detractors, is simply, they are important. Wall Street is akin to the Empire in *Star Wars*. Scew with them and the Empire will strike back.

Wall Street used to be synonymous with power and influence back in the day, when J.P. Morgan was bailing out the United States government in 1907. Now however banks such as Goldman Sachs, Morgan Stanley, and J.P.Morgan have become poster children for incompetency and excess. Yet no one stops to think of the positives. They employ millions of people and combined hold trillions of dollars. This money is your money that they hold, from the input of your salary and compensation to the home or car loan you have with them. Yet people still don't appreciate them. Why? Because as a country we have become a nation of hypocrites. People who consistently change their point of view to the fit the norm. We also are now a confederation of dunces in which the ability to think and speak has gone out the window. As Americans, we take many things for granted, but we always seem to criticize Wall St. The thought that if a bank did not exist, usually never crosses one mind. As a philosophical conundrum, I ask you what would you do with your money if Wall Street did not exist? Would you hide it under the mattress? Or find interesting ways to use it quickly and efficiently. Yet in today's society, the use of credit and debit cards have become the norm. Would you carry in your wallet 50 dollars for groceries each time? Many also use the banks for loans. How would you pay for your house that you are currently living in? The car you drive? These are things we will never have to think about unless we back off Wall Street. The lack of faith is appalling in this country, with the change in view as quick as the single click on a remote control. We take for granted companies like Apple and Microsoft for computing needs. We take for granted companies like Kraft and Pfizer for daily necessities. But we never stop to realize that if the companies we place so much faith in shut down, it would cause a major switch in our daily activities. These companies that Americans have deemed to be an "American Tradition" all became the global powers they are because of Wall Street. As traders and investors told their clients that Apple's idealogy would revolutionize the world people started to buy shares of Apple. This then led to middle America to do the exact same. What is also appalling is the fact that the numbers of Americans who claim to be educated with Master's and Ph.D.s have failed to see something quite obvious. I, a young adult can clearly see exactly what is wrong with the United States and understands who should actually be put under a microscope.

WALL ST VS THE LOWER CLASS

What defines a man? The money of Bill Gates? The looks of George Clooney? Honestly, I have no idea. For the average man the combination of money and looks that they seemingly lack culminates to a place with a "river at one end and a graveyard at another." A place in one of the richest parts of the world with a population of about 1,600,000 and average income upward of $100,000. Wall Street. The Love-Hate relationship that the Street conjures is an image of a many headed monster whose only purpose is to screw one out of his hard earned money. The low income people of the United States comprise about (15.1%) of the population. Their (the Urban poor) view of the "monster" is limited due to their belief that the hard earned $12,000 dollars they make is taxed at 6% by Uncle Sam. This money is then given to banks as they hold Treasury bonds or as part of the Troubled Asset Relief Program bailout. They believe that the fairest way for everyone to become equal is for the banks to start giving money away in droves to the point that the banks go out of business. The problems with this idea are:

1. Banks will have less money thus less buying power.

2. By having controlled cash flow the financial institutions that are pushing mediocrity in the market right now will see a decline in stock price.

3. If the economy is doing badly then the poor people will most likely be out of a job, however the "chain reaction" is that if the economy is doing well then salaries will increase.

4. No Wall Street firms and no New York Stock Exchange means the Western Hemisphere is useless.

5. Wall Street firms globally account for 8% of the world's working population.

6. If Wall Street doesn't exist your employer cannot afford to pay you your current salary. For that matter a salary at all.

7. When you are jobless the government can't give you unemployment because they can't tax the rich bankers.

8. Poverty will rise exponentially.

As instructed by the government the Wall Street firms were ordered to give mortgages to anyone regardless of financial situation. Wall Street questioned how someone making $12,000 a year could afford a $300,000 home without going into debt. That is why the government needed to bail out AIG and thus prevent further home foreclosures. Following the bailout that they received from the government, many in the public were calling them "The Devil" (clear breach of the media bias) after AIG gave "bonuses" to their employees. The word bonus should have been replaced with salary. AIG needed the money in order to pay their employees. If they didn't get paid AIG could have been.

- •Sued

- • Or had their employees jump ship
    - As this would have been in nobody's best interest, AIG did what it had to do.

Despite the bailout, Nancy Pelosi decided to give taxpayer money to things such as $200,000 for the study of bees or the $4,400,000 given to North Carolina Schools for the Board of Education to improve the Math and literacy skills for teachers. Why? I have no clue. But if she doesn't care where the money is going, why should anybody else? Instead of degrading Wall Street we should have an Occupy Pelosi's lawn movement. At the rate at which ranking House and Senate Democrats and Republicans are chastising Wall Street, the only feasible economic system that they will approve of will be one used during the Industrial Revolution. With another U.S. Steel monopoly run by a robber baron and children working and getting their hands cut off for seven cents an hour. While, simultaneously, their fathers work for the entire day and get paid maybe fourteen cents an hour. At that rate in order to buy a gallon of milk it would take two days of fourteen hour labor. But thank you Barney Frank, because I have a job. So now our economy is healthy. In 2008 as people saw that Lehman Brothers was going to fail they realized that the smaller companies that they were working for would be next. Small business owners started filing for Chapter 11 Bankruptcy in order to prevent being taken to the grave. Larger companies started letting millions of workers go until they were right sized. Had the government stepped in and saved Lehman: millions of jobs and money would have been saved. The problem with the government is that they fail to see the big picture because instead of listening to Wall Street they decided that they should play the part of Batman and attempt to save Gotham. Instead, they actually played the part of a literal joker. By this I mean leave the economics to Wall Street, the place where people who studied economics work (see the syllogism there). By not letting the people who went to business school and have a degree in Economics deal with the economics, and instead by forcing their hand upon everything. The people who majored in lying to people A.K.A. The House Committee on Financial Services in college are now handling the economy. The irony is that they have no idea of how to do it. Hey, Uncle Sam, if you want to help America, show Wall Street respect, and give them a chance to do what they went to school to do. The difference between my book and everybody else's is that I care what Wall Street thinks about the poor. The hate of the poor was at its climax following the meltdown of 2008 when 3 major firms went under for sub-prime mortgages. Yet when Wall Street was hurting did anybody try and help. No. The irony is as a race we demand something from the rich, yet the system does not work both ways. For example have you ever seen Oprah or 60 Minutes do a show about a rich guy who became poor? No. No one wants to hear about someone who owned three Ferraris and one bad deal caused him to become instantaneously poor. In Hollywood terms the script does not sell. People want to hear about the guy who lives in Grand Central foraging for food to feed his family. They want to feel a connection to people like that in order to fulfill themselves. America has a natural tendency to fall for sob stories and the poor know how to milk it. This ironically creates a paradox because let's face it as a race we need money to survive. Yet when Wall Street is giving money charitably no one gives a damn and instead everyone thinks that the firms are doing it so they can screw the government out of additional tax revenue . However, at the same time when a doctor gives someone in Africa pills they become *Time's* Person of the Year when both are giving their patients/clients what they need. This seems unfair. Just because the doctor tells people he wants to "help" others doesn't make it more impressive than giving suitcases full of cash to charity. The other problem that exists is any retaliation against the poor would cause a major public relations problem the likes of which the world has never seen before. The poor don't give a damn about other people's hard earned money. I mean this makes a lot of sense such that you don't have respect for something you have never had a lot of. It's just like owning a car in Manhattan, you would not ever use it, and in fact there are many hassles with just owning a car in New York City. However, someone in Texas probably couldn't go a day without a car. The firms don't need the poor with their 30 year fixed mortgage worth 100 grand. Those are pennies for firms. The idea that the poor frequently bypass is when you need money you logically go to a bank. Where am I going to get 10,000 dollars for this car I want to buy when the banks turn me away? Thus illustrating that money controls people. And Wall Street controls money ergo Wall Street controls people. Veni, Vidi Vici. In all fairness the gap between the Street and the poor is one that makes a lot of sense. Both are used to different things. Wall Street commands the mentality of a winner and the ability to take risks. The poor are used to a buy one get one free deal at Wal-Mart. Wall Street doesn't hate them for being poor. That's life, you win some and you lose some. The hate is in the fact that these brokers worked their ass off at one point in their life to get to where they are now. While these poor people looking for handouts reminds them of what they could have become. It is a bad version of nostalgia.

Middle class, you complain about the bailout; look at the amount of money spent by Congress on poor people.

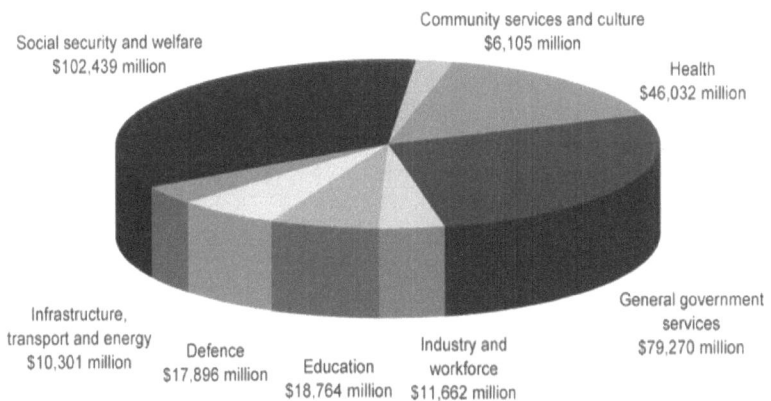

Wall Street also like anybody else in the world hates paying taxes. Yet because of numerous government sponsored "welfare" plans such as Medicaid and Social Security (See Above), Wall Street is paying upwards of billions of dollars on poor people, because they couldn't keep a job. These programs contribute annually to expenditures of trillions of taxpayer dollars. Money that comes from every person paying taxes regardless of social class. Instead of getting on Wall Street's asses about how mean and greedy they are (it's not true), why not get on the poor people's asses about getting a job so these programs can go bye-bye? Along those same lines all the wellness programs are not only sponsored by taxpayer money. They are helped by selling bonds which Wall Street firms buy. Thus directly Wall Street is helping out the little guy.

WALL ST VS. THE MIDDLE CLASS

The middle class is a thorn in Wall Street's side. All of this began when the housing bubble crashed in 2007 and the government implemented measures that allowed mortgages to be given to people who couldn't afford it. This forced banks to foreclose on defaulting homeowners and left the banks with assets that were depreciating very quickly. This led to massive debt and eventually led to the failure of three big banks, Bear Stearns, Lehman Brothers, and Merrill Lynch. This is the main reason Wall Street hates the middle class. They believe that the middle class screwed them and then hypocritically tried to blame them for "excess" and "greed." Instead of apologizing, the middle class decided to start occupying 90% of the already –small island of Manhattan. The hate of banking started in *Merchant of Venice* when Shakespeare portrayed Shylock as a greedy son-of-a-bitch, and it is still going on today. People frequently forget Wall Street's purpose of raising capital and growing business. The middle class's view of people in corner offices, drinking whiskey at 2 in the afternoon, wearing three thousand dollar Armani Suits is erroneous. Now that's not to say they aren't better than you. They are. Yet, no one appreciates being called names especially the people on Wall Street who have been given a reputation as being greedy, when in actuality nothing is further from the truth. If anything Wall Street views the middle class as greedy, because generally they are not satisfied with anything. Some of the middle class then try market timing. One has a higher chance of winning both the lottery and being struck by lightning in the same life than of timing the market correctly. Webster defines "greed" as a selfish and excessive desire for more of something (as money) than is needed. The middle class is greedy; use of coupons by the middle class accounts for 3.7 billion dollars saved a year. Now with that extra money they can go buy something else which will eventually, over time, allow for amassing more wealth. That sounds akin to the definition of greed to me. Money is an important thing. It facilitates transactions and stores value. It controls. It defines people. To fit this phenomena *Forbes* releases a list called Most Outrageous CEO's every year which details compensation for that year. Towards the top of that list is usually Goldman Sachs Chief Executive Officer, Lloyd Blankfein somewhere around 20 million dollars. Now for those people who think that is high for a banker, you're wrong. I am going to tell you a little known fact: Goldman Sachs in 2008 reported a loss of about 35 billion compared to Merrill Lynch's 45 and Bank of America's, 80 Billion. In 2009 Goldman reported record profits. They went from worst to first in a year that was by no means lenient for any financial institution. While Bank of America and Citigroup were losing revenue Blankfein and Goldman prospered, actually posting a profit. That's why he was paid accordingly. Goldman was making money like nobody's business. Once again thanks to Blankfein. Thanks to Blankfein he should be compensated in a just way because he pulled off an impressive feat. To illustrate this better I will tell another personal anecdote.

When I was six, I went to a party hosted by my dad's colleague. Over dinner they were discussing how many of them had lost most of their savings due to Dot-Com bubble burst. I unknowingly- yet with an air of curiosity-asked them how much money they made as to ascertain the extent to which these people lost. At this point everybody just looked at me like a jackass. I now know that it is in poor taste to do that. Getting to my point, while I do not personally know Lloyd Blankfein, I am pretty sure he doesn't appreciate random jackasses commenting on how much money he makes. Let me put it into a life lesson that everyone gets taught. If you don't want it to happen to you then don't do it to others. I am positive he doesn't go around asking about your meager salary, and proclaim it to the world. Despite making 100 times what you do.

As I was talking to one of my Wall Street friends his cell-phone rang and his client wanted to discuss an investment worth about 35 million dollars. However the market was down, and he was unsure as to whether certain stocks were good buys. My friend assured him it was all well and that he should buy. I later asked my friend when the market is down who gets on you? His reply, the middle class. This made me curious. His rebuttal was that high net worth people understand the cyclical nature of the stock market. The middle class, he explained had limited money to invest so rationally when markets tank they freak easily. On the same topic he also stated that the middle class is off his ass when the market is in la-la land where nobody can do any wrong. Yet when the markets goes to the dogs, even a loss of 50 points, his firm gets a call from someone freaking. He told me he attributed this to lack of knowledge of the market. He stated the rich do their homework. He also was complaining about how these people don't really understand what is going on. Because of this they complain constantly and try and tell these people how to do their jobs. Eventually that only gets you a pissed off banker; who is not gracious when speaking to you. Additionally, the middle class consistently complains about Wall Street and their no care attitude for their actions. This complaint is especially true of Investment bank, Goldman Sachs. Whenever you hear about some scandal on Wall Street the press is generally referring to them. Yet what people don't know is that Goldman is very charitable. They have started a charity called 10,000 Small Businesses because they do care about the middle class despite the paradox.

- 10,000 Small Businesses

"A 500 million dollar initiative that will unlock the growth and job creation potential of 10,000 small businesses." They have divided up the money to go to local business schools in the hope that scholarships can be offered to small business owners. The program will allow the owners learn the ins and outs of running a small business. The curriculum will be thought up by people at the leading business schools i.e. Wharton, HBS. Goldman will then give the other 300 million dollars to community development financial institutions. This will allow people in underappreciated neighborhoods the chance to accrue some capital as well as get help trying to find other sources of capital. And the cherry on top is that Goldman will personally brokerage these small businesses and provides the right advice in order to head them in the right way.

- 10,000 Women

As Goldman sees it, women are the true innovators and leaders of tomorrow. Thus Goldman allows women who are in a disadvantaged background the ability to come and learn courses in business in order to further their knowledge and help them with their business careers.

- Goldman Sachs Gives

This is the biggest and most important of their charities. It has been set up into four categories.

1. Service Veterans

Goldman has created a "mission" where they provide veterans with community service positions to allow them to assimilate into civilian life. Goldman also provides counseling options.

2. Economic Growth

In order to get youth acquainted with business, Goldman has given 1.5 million dollars for teenagers to get a job working in a business, and learning the tools of the trade.

3. Community Growth

Goldman is driven in order to provide funding for new schools and after school play areas. This attracts more people to the community and allows for growth.

They help and give because they want to make a difference, and many don't realize that. Yes, Wall Street has quite a bit of power, but it also is trying to help for tomorrow's world. They want to build the people who will eventually run this country. Now do you still think Wall Street doesn't care, every firm has their own version of charities with JPMorgans's Pathways to Opportunity and Citigroup's Citi Foundation.

There exists due to the financial meltdown a misguided hate that should be moved from Wall Street to people like Chris Dodd and Nancy Pelosi who, thanks to their self-appointed Economics degrees, really screwed a lot of stuff up. Wall Street has been taking crap from everyone when they were trying to do the right thing. By helping out the little guy Wall Street did indeed profit but so did you. Yet now you do nothing as they are hammered by the Securities and Exchange Commission for "questionable practices?" If someone screws me like that I am going to be careful of trusting again. The reason though that Wall Street has been taking crap for years by the middle class is the fact that the government said so. Have any of them come out and truly apologized? No. Why should they? They have perhaps the greatest scapegoat of all time. By trying to help out the little guy, Wall Street firms ended with billions of dollars of debt. This led to a 250 billion dollar bailout by the government to prevent a catastrophe. The irony is the government threw taxpayer money Wall Street's away in order to cover up their mistakes. Wall Street was and still is entitled to this money, because we saw what happened when a bank failed. The markets to some extent are still reeling. So Wall Street believes that instead of picketing we should all go to Washington and start camping out on Capitol Hill. We should start demanding answers from the government as to why Americans are unemployed. The government wants stronger regulation of banks for one reason, to cover their asses. This is all bull.

The middle class believe that they are the backbone of the economy and they dislike Wall Street, because Wall St. has been "supposedly" taking their jobs. In truth Wall Street was trying to help and it was the fault of the government. It's not just their fault alone. The middle class can't keep up due to their outrageous spending habits. In fact, I know a man who makes 85 thousand dollars a year. He owns a 40 thousand dollar BMW and a 350 thousand dollar home. How he pays his bills is beyond me. These people don't understand how much debt they have. When the bank forecloses it becomes "Blame Wall Street for my lack of common-sense."

The middle class also has a problem with Wall Street due to the belief that they work harder as employees. This is not true. A Wall Street workday is typically like this

1. 5 AM: wake up
2. 7 AM: get to work
3. 10 PM: come home from work
4. 5 AM: next day wake up to go to work

A typical day in an office building

1. 7:30 AM: wake up
2. 9 AM: get to work
3. 12 PM-1 PM: lunch break

4. 5-6 PM: leave to go home
5. 6-10 PM: family time
6. 10 PM: bed time

Obviously it is clear that no one works harder than a banker. A Wall Street career is glamorous. But with glamour comes a boatload of hard work, i.e. an athlete plays for only 6 months in a year at most, but the other 6 months, he/she must practice. Hard work begets success.

Lawsuits have been the face of America for some time, you don't like someone you sue them, you need money you sue them, we have even gone so far as to sue doctors. The people who save our live so we can live to sue another day. Yet, it's a known fact that people sue banks, because they have a lot of money. There was recently a lawsuit by a group of middle class investors against banking giant Bank of America. These "investors" purchased mortgages on Bank of America's mortgage lender Countrywide Financial. As these homeowners defaulted on their mortgages because they lost their jobs, the investors are suing Bank of America on the basis that they lost their home due to Countrywide not adequately stating the risk involved. Bull! Due to credit being accessible so easily, at the time I would have been a 13 year old kid with maybe 100 bucks and a winning smile to my name, I could have gotten credit on an 80 thousand dollar house (Not really, but you get my point). The risks would have definitely been defined. Bank of America is a member of both the FDIC and FINRA, which means they legally are required to disclose risk. Ergo this case is questionable at best. And, these investors are morons and are just trying to pin their stupidity on somebody else. Bank of America –out of the goodness of their heart-decided to shell out 600 million dollars in order to help some of the people in May 2010. The people who are now suing Bank of America had the chance of free capital, but instead said no. They would rather try and fight this out in court. Some of you may be facing a similar decision. Take a second and think -- did anybody force you to buy an overpriced house? My point is that suing Wall Street is not going to take away from the fact of public laughter. This is one of the nicer suits against the Street. And let me stress the fact that you could have Harvey Spector, Clarence Darrow, or even Atticus Finch as your lawyer, but you will lose.

WALL STREET AND THE RICH

What does being rich mean? A 90210 zip code? A Ferrari in the driveway? A butler named Jeeves? The idea of being rich has been ingrained in America. It makes sense. Money begets power. Money begets respect. But most of all money begets fame. But what does that have to do with Wall Street? Wall Street is a dream weaver; they can make anybody rich. By doing so many of these people who became rich form friendships with their Financial advisers/money managers.. In fact my parents' money manager has said countless number of times that you become more than friends with your clients, you become their confidantes. You know more about their families than they know about their own.

Yet people despise the rich and Wall Street because of their wealth. Why? They help bolster Aggregate Demand by consuming countless number of things they do not need. In fact in order to fix the problems created by the lower classes Wall Street and their rich buddies have:

1. Started buying
They are trying to help you. Do not be hypocritical about it and rub it in their face that you think that they are making too much and should be guillotined. More spending= more consuming=more jobs=economic growth and stability.

2. Create Jobs
They own business that put you to work.

3. Tax allocation

Alert to the world, even with recession rich people are still rich. In fact, the amount of luxury goods being purchased right now has never been higher. Money will keep flowing through, but out of the goodness of their hearts the rich and Wall Street have started buying everything from household goods to treasury bonds. This allows the government to:

*   Pay for civil services such as Medicaid, Social Security and Unemployment
*   Can inflate the money supply in order to ease the recession

The rich aren't expecting extravagant help on this but when Wal-Mart has a two for one sale on milk go buy. Macroeconomics 101, more consumption leads to a shift rightward of the Aggregate Demand curve.

I apologize to all the hard working middle class Americans (note the sarcasm) but if Wall Street closed shop tomorrow we are all screwed. The thing you need to realize is that you need Wall Street, they don't need you. In fact, I was reading an article written by a banker detailing why Wall Street will never die. His argument albeit written quite viciously had some points that truly can sum up what happens if Wall Street and the rich keep being chastised. They can

- Fire the people who work for them i.e. maids, gardeners and do the work themselves

- Eventually because of their over qualification they will start taking jobs, such as "teaching 3rd graders." They will be overqualified people doing less than glamorous jobs because they have been through the hardship of working. They know exactly what it feels like

- They are used to working around the clock and working under pressure

- Eventually as their income comes down so will their spending. And the free rides on their coat tails will no longer be available

The top Americans cost the United States 41 cents per dollar. The bottom Americans cost the government $8.21 per dollar a difference of $7.80. There are 300 million Americans and about a fifth are rich. This means 24,6000,00 dollars of the government's money is spent. But the lower classes cost the government about 985,200,000 dollars. The middle class costs the government $1.30 which comes about to 156,000,000 dollars. The government doesn't have that kind of money. So that's where the rich come in. Thus to bridge the gap they are taxed more. Which mind you, is still not enough, which is why we are in debt right now. The rich account for just about over 50% of federal income tax paid. That's the top1% of Americans who pay for about 150 million people.

Ever think what the definition of a banker is? A banker is one engaged in the business of receiving other people's money in deposit. That's every single person who has ever handled money. We exchange money. We budget money. We lend money. We invest money. By this very sound logic, we do the exact same thing Wall Street does except on a smaller level. The irony is self-evident.

I have always been told that friendship between Wall Street and the rich is best learned through stories of a young investment banker with a choice and the CEO who had the life of his friend in his hand.

There once were two friends who had graduated HBS together. Josh who had aspirations of working on Wall Street was somewhat of a slacker and James however was a hardworking straight A student who always gave 110%. So both friends graduated and went their separate ways, but still kept in touch, till one day James now CEO of a fortune 500 company decided that he wanted to purchase a smaller company in order to enlarge the company. He approached Josh who was a successful Investment banker about doing this merger. However, what James did not know about Josh is that he had just bought a new apartment and needed some money in order to pay his mortgage. Because of this Josh knew that this deal needed to go through because it would net his firm 85 billion dollars and earning him a bonus that would help him buy the house. Josh also knew that the company that James wanted to buy had a dark secret that it was actually harboring some of the worst financial statements in company history and buying them would surely oust James from the position he loved so much. Josh was in a dilemma so he called his other friend, Hank who he had met a couple of years ago while working abroad in London who was the epitome of the middle class. They talked and Hank advised him to take the deal because James would always find another job. Still wanting to get another opinion Josh called his other friend Harry who lived in the middle of nowhere Texas. The thing about Harry was that he was a very successful businessman with his company spanning the entire world. Harry advised him to not take the deal because he had been screwed by a merger and it had messed up his relationship with his parents who had died in a car accident following that. Finally Josh went to his boss, Jim, head of investment banking for the last bit of advice. Jim was a caring family man who had a vocabulary like a sailor, but was deemed the "Godfather" of Wall Street for he had helped his firm's investment banking division grow tenfold since his arrival 34 years ago. Josh began to explain the situation when Jim held his hand up took a piece of paper from the printer and wrote something on a post- it handed the page to Josh and left the room.

Josh was puzzled, but he looked down and there was a spreadsheet that Josh had given him earlier detailing 2nd quarter profits however when Josh reexamined the page he noticed that there was an extra column detailing the numbers if the merger went through and Josh was astounded to see that the revenue would go up by 10% an astounding number which according to the spreadsheet would net Josh a million dollar bonus which included performance and profits from the merger more than enough to buy this house and an engagement ring for his soon to be fiancé, Melissa. However Josh also read the post- it and attached to it were four words barely legible under that chicken scratch that Jim called handwriting "Is it worth it?" In financial terms it was a killer. Josh knew that from this he could get promoted very quickly. Yet he had a vision into the future with his friend James rattling on his door begging him to let him in from the winter's cold embrace wearing the shirt he had when he was left behind by the world, carrying a box of a bunch of useless memories. Josh knew what he had to do, he had to in a sense save his friend's soul from being sold to the devil. Josh quickly pulled out his phone and dialed his friend's number. As James picked up the phone Josh explained the situation to him and James quickly conferenced with his company's board of directors after explaining the situation to them they too agreed to call It quits on the merger. The next day as Josh was walking to work, James called in order to tell him thank you. On the way Josh met Jim who asked him how it went and Josh explained what had transpired. Jim then stated the "phrase of the century" through to this very day sticks with Josh. "Money is great, but friendship is greater."

There were two friends named Michael and Fred who both worked at the same Investment bank on Wall Street in the late eighties. Michael had just created the junk bond market, a bond with a high risk high reward. Fred was the CEO of a company that was challenging the likes of Goldman Sachs and Merrill Lynch for top dog on Wall Street The thing that made Fred and Michael such good friends is that the money that Fred had made was thanks to Michael, and he returned the favor by allowing Michael to manage his portfolio. The difference between Michael and Fred was that Michael was carefree while Fred was a strict down to the book kind of guy. Their company was notable for being more aggressive than most especially in the case of mergers, investments, and others. This however, against main stream Wall Street culture led some of these men into the "deep" end. However, the firm started on a downfall following the allegations of an insider trading conspiracy of a newly hired employee who was described as the typical middle class man. The Securities and Exchange Commission (SEC) later sued the firm due to a tip from a man who had worked with the insider trading scandal. Fred believed this case was brought against the firm in order to prevent jail time for those involved in the insider trading scandal. Yet Fred was shocked when the SEC charged Michael with insider trading. The SEC was threatening with a Racketeer Influenced and Corrupt Organizations Act (RICO), and Fred knew if they were indicted they would be screwed. Fred decided that Michael was innocent and as his friend would have never done anything like that, he decided to fight these allegations. However, then a lawyer for the state of New York named Rudy decided to go ahead and sue. Fred knew that the firm's reputation could be seriously hurt if this went to trial, so he refused to acknowledge that anything had happened. However as Fred had predicted investors started doubting Fred and his firm and their stock declined to the point that Fred had to cut 5000 jobs, yet that wasn't enough, and as the firm headed for bankruptcy Fred split up the company into two entities that could last alone, and today that is exactly what happened as on February 13th 1990 Drexel Burnham Lambert filed for Chapter 11 Bankruptcy, on the grounds that Fred Joseph who had made money beyond his wildest imagination thanks to Michael Milken went to bat for him, forgetting about the company but refusing to lose a friend.

When the rich and Wall Street sit down in a New York penthouse wearing stuffy suits and drinking wine discussing how much better they are than everybody else. Sorry that's a Dickens novel. Just like the friendship between you and your best friends that's how it is, it's just about friendship and not about the money.

WALL STREET AND FOREIGN MARKETS

Instrumental? What does it mean in terms of business? How does it function? Who is instrumental? To answer that question one has got to look at Wall Street and its relationship with people working on foreign markets. Wall Street believes them to be instrumental in that:

1.   Keeping the world economy running smoothly

As we saw in 2008 by the falling of 3 financial sectors giants the world economy is still in a rut. Yet had it not been for these people working on foreign markets we would be in far worse shape. They were able to prevent a global slide into a depression which allowed for most of you to keep your jobs from the mess that Uncle Sam created. So you can tip your hat to them. Even on good days these people are instrumental in keeping countries' economies running as smoothly as possible.

2.   Produce revenue for the banks

"Outsourced" financial institutions account for 18% of annual profit. If these banks did not exist then places like Goldman Sachs and Deutsche Bank could possibly go out of business.

3.   Impractical for trading from 30 different countries to happen on the same trading floor

Imagine working in a small confined space the size of a small cubicle and fitting 300 hundred people in there. Something you would see at the circus. Right? That would be the exact same if you had a bunch of traders discussing different markets six feet away it would lead to confusion. Additionally when dealing with investors it is preferable to have close contact with them. Something that cannot be accomplished if they are in China and you are in New York City.

4.   Allows them to do their job (I can't stress this enough)

These people don't have to worry about the office politics involved, and can truly focus on two things: the markets and the investors. They also don't have to deal with the press about how maybe such and such looks on a downturn and whether they recommend buying. They also don't have to worry about being badgered 24/7 with people telling them that they are cruel and heartless for working on Wall Street

5. Gain understanding to the people that use these markets

Let's say I am working with investors in Dubai it helps tenfold. By meeting these people one can gain the knowledge of what they like to invest in, their level of risk, where they want to be in twenty years. By learning stuff like this, Wall Street firms can learn about what they can do to help, such as invest money in mutual funds or stocks.

6. It helps Wall Street expand in terms of location

Imagine if you lived in a place that was far away from your brokerage firm and a bunch of people who also used the same brokerage firm lived in your area. It would only make sense that Wall Street would open up a location in your area.

7. Very helpful for investors

They generally have a higher growth rate which an investor can see his/her investment grow tenfold in a shorter amount of time.

8. Important to keep a good record on them

Many nations are dependent on the U.S. economy and vice versa, by this virtue when foreign markets outperform, a bad day on the New York Stock Exchange is well not as bad. That's why Wall Street pays so much importance to foreign markets

9. Money

Developing nations are a haven for investors as they can see infrastructure rise and their stock prices rise as well as the economy become bigger. See, Coke in China is for the rich and upper middle class, there are not very many of them. As China's economy grows, Coke becomes more accessible to the masses and thus allows for Coke's revenue and ultimately profit and stock price to rise through the roof.

10. Equities

The equity markets in foreign countries have steadily grown and will continue to grow, a well sought out fund or stock could be the key to a huge amount of money and financial security for Wall Street's clients.

FOREIGN MARKETS AND WALL STREET

Emotions are what drive mankind. Can you imagine a world where no emotion was felt? Sounds depressing, right? WRONG, a world with no emotion would be quite successful. Why? The lack of being able to think of business as only business is something I dream of. See especially for foreigners, Wall Street stands only as business, and nothing more. To them they see it as just a trading floor where deals happen. They see it as management not trying to play office politics. Why? Because in countries such as England, India and Japan business is a game of respect. Ironically, something we as a nation lack.

It's 3:30 in the afternoon you walk into any Wall Street. firm in Nariman Point in Mumbai, India you are greeted with a nice smile, a newspaper, and a cup of coffee. You are then politely asked to go through the lobby adorned with sculptures and paintings of Hindu deities showing Indian traditionalist views of business as one governed by God. As you go up the elevator you can clearly see the view that these firms have of what they do. The elevator is bland denoting that these firms are open for business and only business. As you enter the trading floor you see traders taking/making calls, you see their secretaries getting them to sign papers simultaneously, and then you see the secretary's secretary going back and forth to the traders' desks to pick up papers. Essentially, Indians are about efficiency and output. You then meet the guy in charge of the floor who combs his way through the traders like John Gutfreund used to do at Salomon Brothers in New York. As the markets wind down for the day and you start heading for the elevator you see colleagues milling around the elevator waiting to leave, but you also notice that these 40 people waiting for the three elevators aren't talking to each other. They come to work to work to them it's just business. See that's how most of the world views Wall Street not as something symbolizing big business, dream takers and every other bad name Americans have given Wall Street over the last 200 years, but as only business and the purpose of business is to expand and grow and be accessible to the average man. This is especially true of such companies like JPMORGAN CHASE which holds the largest number of personal banking clients in the world has now gone to countries all around the world from South Africa to China. Why can't we be like the Asians in our work ethic? I mean let's face it ten years from now China or India will be the biggest economy in the world. Why? Because instead of having to deal with constant criticism from people who don't like their jobs these people should go suck it up and work hard because increasing productivity means two things

- Bigger and better are coming for you

Sure you may hate your job now, but if you keep working hard you can get promoted and keep rising in the ranks and then you will become part of America's elite. Then your outlook on this whole situation will change.

- Bigger and better for the economy

But I digress once again though based on numbers from 2010 JPMORGAN offices in India have accounted for 1 billion plus over a market boom that started in 1999 so on average about a million dollars a year in revenue from investment banking for JPM. However had the US gone way of the Indian's back in 1884 when Charles Dow first started trading his 11 railroad stocks then hypothetically USA JPM revenue from investment banking would be around somewhere in the 120 million dollar mark without factoring inflation instead of the measly 17 million dollars. However don't get me wrong JP MORGAN is the most successful investment banking not only in Asia, but in the world all together. So props for that. Anyway the 2nd largest market in the world China boasts a 5.6 billion dollar revenue for JPM over an economy that since 1990 has grown at an amazing rate and averages about 2.8 million dollars a year or in the 116 year history of Wall Street about 325 million dollars alone. Now is this likely to happen 100% not, but imagine instead of 17 million dollars JPM made 325 million dollars, the economy would have the biggest jump since the days of the new deal, and thus create jobs for everyone i.e. JPM stock price goes up, then the investing companies win they then use the money to create more jobs and then those new people working will need to hire people to take care of kids, mow the lawn, etc. thus creating jobs. Especially those in the financial sector from UBS to Deutsche Bank, because everyone will want to get in on this explosion that will rival the gold rush. If we as Americans can change our ways and stop being so emotional about Wall Street and stop complaining constantly. Wall Street secretaries can stop telling their boss that Capitol Hill called, then the office politics can stop. Then Wall Street can lead the charge to the future. (OK, that was corny but you get the point.) If business starts becoming about emotion, soon the U.S. economy will not be able to survive getting left in the dust by countries like China, Japan, and India. Furthermore, what's even worse is as a country we are getting laughed at by others for "being too close" to something so pointless. Want proof? As I was visiting family in India, I went to the bank that my uncle works at where I asked him about what he thought of the class warfare between Americans and Wall Street He believed it to be:

- Juvenile

India has enough problems and having to deal with class warfare is not one of them. Indians also believe talking about stuff like that is crass. They also believe that as a company the Wall Street firms are doing exactly what they should be doing: making money for their clients and expanding business. There is not a single sane person in the world who does not like making money. It's what we were born to do. Many foreigners laugh at the American people, because by attempting to hold big business back, we are just going to become even more dependent on foreign nations.

- Typical of Americans

It's very typical of Americans to hold grudges; in fact part of the Civil War was based on a grudge of the North having more political power. What makes this any different? Americans hate Wall Street because it is typical of Americans to hate people who are quite different than they are. People hate the visionaries, and Wall Street is the lead in today's world. Nothing escapes the watchful eye of Wall Street's analysts. When Google went public, there were skeptics but Wall Street encouraged people to buy and of those who did they are doing very well.

- Wrong when compared to the other problems in this country

My uncle had a very true point with this when he said compared to the other problems in this country from unemployment to poverty. By adding this unnecessary problem, instead of being able to find ways to reduce foreign dependence, policymakers are going to instead find ways of trying to cover up their screw ups. When all of this could be avoided by letting Wall Street do as it pleases, mind you Wall Street has led us since the start of the DJIA in 1884.

- It's about something else, not the class hate

My uncle also hit on the point that it is about more than just hate. It's truly about jealousy and awe. Jealousy in the fact that Wall Streeters live a Vegas lifestyle in the risk taking, exhilaration, and enjoyment of playing with money. Jealousy of the compensation they get at the end of the year despite not knowing the working conditions of these super heroes in suits (and they truly are.) Think a less attractive and funny Robert Downey, Jr. 's "alter ego" Tony Stark. In awe of "perfect" businessman one who is dressed for success, works hard, and excels at what he does. In awe of the men and women who constantly shape Americas future.

- We haven't evolved since the Colonial period

In Colonial times it was customary for the Colonial elite to be part of the "In crowd" of people who were mainly bankers and landowners. Throughout that time many become jealous of the bankers only cautiously giving money to people they knew could afford to pay it back. In this time it was customary for the men to be shop owners i.e. blacksmiths, carpenters etc. Since many times bankers would not give them money due to the knowledge that they wouldn't be able to pay it back (today though that is not the case as we saw in 08) discontentment grew. In 1775 at the onset of the Revolutionary War all that was put away in order to fight the British, however with the onset of political parties, the discontentment has grown. And it has escalated to what it is today with slander by the middle class, and the pointing of fingers. So truly my uncle was right for a country that has seen nothing but bright days for the last half century with the advent of the computer, endeavors by Apple, and voyages into space, we truly have not grown and seen our ancestors' view of America, one with liberty and justice for all.

If we get left in the dust by those countries we have only ourselves to blame because we would have brought this upon ourselves and our children will be forced to pay for our misdeeds.

WALL STREET AND ITS EMPLOYEES

Utopia is defined as an ideal community with a perfect political and social system. Many have attempted to find such a place and failed miserably. Most notably Sir Thomas More. Yet according to Dante, Paradise can be found. While not the sunny beaches of Florida, Paradise is every floor of a Wall Street bank. What makes it so utopian and lovely? Well,

- Just another way of life

What's the difference between someone going to work in a factory vs. someone on Wall Street? Nothing! Both get jobs because they need the money, just like the rest of America. Sure there is some glamor, but at the end of the day it is just another job. Albeit, with hours that are hellish, and the last thing anyone wants is to deal with after having worked 80 hours a week is people questioning you.

- Compensation

The entertainment business has become the face of America for quite some time. Outsiders can see only the glamor, the money, and the exotic lives these people are living. Nobody sees the 14-18 hour workdays, the amount of preparation that goes into a movie (2-3 years). That's why these actors and actresses can afford 10 + million dollar homes, they put tons of effort and time into giving a top notch performance, so they are paid accordingly. However the most profitable business in America is the financial sector. Why? These people put in hours that are unheard of, they sleep at work after working till 3a.m., they are constantly on call etc. Ever worked like that? Didn't think so. Many have a problem with the amount that they get paid. To that I say

- Screw You
- Try working like that for one week, it'll drive you crazy.

That's why come January Wall Street becomes utopian because it is bonus season, and everyone wants to see the work they put in compensated properly.

The problem with America is that as a country we see results, and don't think any more about them. i.e. Morgan Stanley makes 32 billion in revenue in 2010 yet we don't or rather refuse to see the amount of work that went into getting there and thus refuse to acknowledge it. Then we become angry because someone makes more money than we do.

- Attracts Top Talents

Imagine if you could work with friends who think and act exactly like you do. Great isn't it? That what makes Wall Street so utopian for all the employees working with people who do can help you grow, due to the same shared interests. I was reading an article about how the middle class is upset at Wall St. for attracting the top talents and I thought it be a great place to interject my opinion

- No one is forced to come to Wall Street they come on their own

- Who are you to tell them that they have to help you with your problem

- Access to people who change America's economy every day

Michael Lewis in his book *Liars Poker* details of how he grew up under the tutelage of Lewis Ranierei, the Salomon Brothers trader who created the gold rush for mortgage bond trading. Ranierei of course with his "baby" became a leader in the American economy with his anti-Wall Stesque appearance. Anyway imagine being able to work with the forefathers to write the constitution or paint with DaVinci. Sounds amazing doesn't it? That's the chance that Wall Streeters get to have working with people who constantly shape and change America's economy.

- It's like college (fun times!)

Remember college, where almost every day you would get drunk and party? You would then take some coffee and go finish studying. Then go take that

Econ exam at 9 a.m. while half asleep. While Wall Street is not like that the atmosphere of being with your friends, laughing at some truly bad jokes. The point of working on Wall Street is that you never lose that youngish feel from college. Take for example Food Friday at Salomon Brothers mortgage trading desk. The traders would buy mounds of food to just stuff themselves, and to feel as Zach Galifianakis puts it a "Wolf Pack." Another one being the race in the Cleveland office of Salomon Brothers which is touched upon in Charles Gasparino's *The Sellout.* Here two brokers raced up the entire flight of stairs that got everyone including legend John Meriwether to bet on the outcome.

- "Vegas Baby!"

The main thing people do when they go to Vegas is gamble, this usually is a once or twice a year thing. What if I were to tell you I know a way you can gamble every day. "Is that something you might be interested in?" Working on Wall Street means you know the ideas of risk taking, the personalities of the people you are dealing with, and of course the game itself. Many Wall Street bosses stress more risk, because well it means more reward, which can then be reinvested in the company and then the remaining is usually pooled together to start some type of charity. But I digress my point is that it is hard leaving Vegas and it's the same on Wall Street, and you almost never lose.

- Atmosphere

A typical trading floor is like the one you would see in a movie, fast-paced and crazy. Many people thrive in a high pressure, no nonsense type of atmosphere with phones ringing constantly, people complaining loudly, and the knowledge that some of the people you are working with are actually crazy. It's why many go into the business, it makes them happy to arrive to work because they know that the moment the come into work the place becomes like a mad house. The atmosphere also doesn't allow for being boredom.

THE EMPLOYEES AND WALL STREET

But don't forget the bonus. The word everyone wants to hear at the end of the year can come in all forms Incentive and Non-Qualified stock options yet none more wanted than a big fat check. Usually this is to show that as a company the employers care about their workers. It is the exact same thing on Wall Street, with bonus meaning the exact same thing. The thing that Wall Street firms want to show their employees is that you may work on Wall Street but at the end of the day we are any other company and we care about our employees just like Walmart and GE. Many Main Streeters complain about the massive amount of bonuses given, for starters it like every other type of bonus is based on company performance/individual performance and type of employee i.e. VP or CEO.

Another way Wall Street firms show that they care is through company allowances such as expense accounts. By allowing their employees to be treated in style when away on business or even on a day to day basis once again Wall Street is showing its appreciation.

There are many a story about the allowances on Wall Street, and many think it to be just there in order to overly compensate Wall Street employees. This is not the case in fact

1. Apparel

Companies such as JP Morgan Chase allow for employee discounts on things from suits all the way to shorts because they value the fact that for the 80 hours a week that is put in by the employees they should be comfortable in their clothes and not have to worry about sitting in an uncomfortable suit all day while trying to work. Albeit they are not.

2. Banking Services

After all, these are banks. For employees if they're in need of cash quickly or due to long hours are unable to cash a check they can do it in the privacy of their own office. They also have direct payroll in order to minimize the amount of time they have to go around searching for a bank. This is done to allow for freedom when the employees have it to do as they please.

3. Employee Arts and Culture Program

This program allows for discounts at major shows, gardens, zoos, etc. This once again is done to maximize the free time of the employee without having to worry about taking enough cash and thus allowing for other things such as dining at a restaurant or shopping.

Companies from Merrill Lynch all the way to Morgan Stanley allow for discounts from new cars to new computers. The list is endless, I only picked a few and this is done in order to:

1. Show appreciation for the amount of work done by employees, many who work over 80 hours a week

2. Prevent top employees from leaving the firm

In order to prevent top employees from leaving the firm as noted in Gasparino's *The Sellout*, Jimmy Cayne, former head of Bear Sterns would offer people pot and the ability to name their title. His view was that people you can become mentally unstable with will never leave you. Other companies also allow use of company cars, expense accounts... the exact same things that your boss has.

WALL STREET VS. THE PRESS

September 29, 2008, a day that will live in infamy. The Dow Jones Industrial Average fell 777 points the biggest drop ever to date, people are scrambling to remove their money from the market, jobs started going one-by-one, fear started to set in about the future. The press points the finger at the many headed monster Wall Street. WHY? It is an easy story, there is no digging involved -- yet the true story involves the government's genius plan of trying to allow everyone the American Dream of owning a house, having kids, a nice house, and a golden retriever. Yet the press pointed the finger at the banks. By trying to help people out they went bankrupt, and they collapsed and the market fell and by doing some act of God they could have prevented all of this. Anyway, the stories are real easy to write about because

- The mass population does not know how the market works

If you went up to a 10,000 people in some big city like Miami and asked them why the market was down today they would respond with some fabricated answer that tried to make them look smart.

Now since I am not a big fan of the press telling me about my stocks. I was curious as to why people would watch Jim Cramer for his actual content(Don't get me wrong that guy is hilarious, and he kicks ass at his job). Then it hit me it involves money, the thing people have killed for. The thing that Economics 101 teaches you, you can't live without money. So whenever the market loses money, the press blames Wall Street because they are essentially in this country the vault. And since money is being lost people start to fall into line and start picketing on Wall Street. Also, the press uses the money to come up with elaborate lies such as the fact that the economy hasn't improved citing statistics that mean nothing. Such as the comparison to the amount of people unemployed in developing countries where every 1 in 8 people have a job; we don't care about that. Anyway, the biggest lie from the press in the last 65 years occurred on November 2nd 1948 when the *Chicago Tribune* caption read "Dewey Beats Truman." I guess this means that my history book must be wrong because as I recall Truman was president until 1953. For lack of a better term "Epic Fail," why should we take anything the press says at face value.

The press also takes shots at Wall Street because they believe themselves to be the champion of the middle class. By writing these cockamamie stories of how Wall Street has screwed people for years they believe that somehow Wall Street is going to change their philosophy of making money and in turn start giving money to every schmuck who asks for it. The main philosophy the press abides by is the idea of bias. They use bias in their very sentences such as, "Are you furious? If not, you should be. The giant financial institutions that make up Wall Street have been bailed out, thanks to trillions of dollars of our money, and are on track to hand out record-breaking multibillion-dollar bonuses while millions of regular folks are hurting." I know this not to be true and this was due to government intervention allowing easier access to credit, thus essentially making it the government's fault (I can't stress this enough). Wall Street was entitled to the "Bailout" money from the Troubled Asset Relief Program. However, when put like that it's quite hard to like Wall Street, yet the problem with American media is it's no longer about the truth and quality of the article. It's about a bunch of people who know nothing about finance trying to get everyone to read their paper.

"Stop telling lies about me and I'll stop telling the truth about you," is said to Shia LeBeouf's character Jacob Moore by Gordon Gekko (Michael Douglas) in Oliver Stone's sequel *Wall Street: Money Never Sleeps*. This quote though sums up everything that Wall Street feels about the press in that press consistently fabricates the truth. i.e. I heard about some radio host who claimed that over half of Goldman Sachs revenue went to employee compensation; that is highly fabricated:

- Goldman Sachs had 2010 revenue of about 40 billion dollars

- Total employee compensation for 2010 was 15.38 billion dollars

- That's about 38% of revenue which is also 5 % less than 2009 and a good 12 percent off at least from the number given by this radio host who knew nothing

- Numbers don't lie people do

The "fudging" of numbers by the media has been going on for quite some time from crazy Wall Street bonuses that according to one paper average about 1.5 million dollars a person (Wall Street wishes) the number is actually around 350,000. People of the world I give you proper proof that the media consistently has it in for Wall Street Now if they have been lying about something that's quite easy to check with one phone call who knows what else they have been fabricating, like the reason that so many Americans don't have a job. The government "cough cough." The press does not understand what it is saying and has made Wall Street dislike them deeply, because they are receiving a bad reputation from for essentially someone on a computer getting these random untrue facts from God knows where.

Recently a renowned newspaper which I will refrain from naming for legal purposes published an article about debt ceilings and how instead of controlling it the government. should just go and lose it. This would mean:

Inflation

Imagine it's 2025, we are on the brink of another economic recession, the outlook looks very bad, and that's exactly what would happen if we listen to this guy and just say "the hell with it." This "author" perhaps does not know about Economics 101 and then can at the same time bash Wall Street about its lack of knowledge. But too much inflation is bad which is exactly what is going to happen if the debt gets blown out of the water.

Cost-push

Eventually in order to keep up with the increase in prices, people demand more money while a company which still needs to function starts cutting jobs in order to lower costs.

Social Unrest

Remember in February of 2011 when you turned on the TV and the only thing anybody was talking about was the social unrest in Egypt. When inflation goes up people in countries with high proportions of lower class people start rebelling and that just leads to conflicts everywhere. The author of this article obviously failed to realize that other countries are dependent on the U.S .economy.

Hyperinflation

Remember the iconic photo from Germany with the woman pushing a cart of bills to the bakery in order to buy a loaf of bread? That's hyperinflation. As hyperinflation goes up the ability to supply goods goes down which results in the value of the dollar becoming useless. Then we travel back in time to saying for that chicken I will give you all my vegetables. It's impractical.

Rise in prices

In order to keep up with the economy, companies change prices which makes it harder for people to purchase goods which leads to a higher poverty rate. Eventually the inflation peaks and begins a steep decline at which point everybody is screwed.

Economic Cycle

Essentially a boom and bust cycle where for a time as inflation grows the markets are doing great and the economy is looking great then boom(no pun intended) people are losing jobs and the economic outlook looks like it did in China in the early 1900s.

Wall Street starts hurting

As the value of the dollar decreases, people become more wary about investing, and this causes more people to sell than buy and drives the market into the dust. Then investors turn to bonds which when in a down market perform rather well, which they then cannot cash in on for another twenty years.

Loss of jobs

When companies have to spend more in order to function, their cash flow becomes limited. When this occurs jobs start disappearing off of monster.com. Then everyone starts picketing on Wall Street for somehow subliminally doing something over which they have no control.

The lack of knowledge has become apparent and then these people who have no idea what the crap they are saying have the audacity to tell Wall Street to take a hike. I can only hope that I have opened your eyes to the real truth and hope you form your own opinions while reading such stories. Wall Street doesn't go on a slander streak of every newspaper in the nation. Yet what if Wall Street where to come to the New York Times office on 8th Avenue and start badgering everybody as to what the next scoop was. I guarantee the editors would not appreciate that. By the same logic Wall Street is telling the press to leave them alone.

WALL STREET VS. THE UNITED STATES GOVERNMENT

It's raining heavily outside. The elevator dings in the lobby and security guard Nathan Langley slowly sits up and cocks his head wondering as to who is in the building at 11:45 p.m. He quickly relaxes when he sees just the janitor walk out. However with the janitor exists one of the biggest government conspiracies dating back to the days of Andrew Jackson. Enter John Dunn, rogue ex-CIA Operative who slowly using a stun gun lodged in his mop takes out Nathan Langley. He then takes the service elevator to the file room, enters the code 6534 and then lets the scanner scan his retina as well as finger. The lights come on signaling that John has been granted access. Then he quickly finds the door conveniently located behind the vending machine that hasn't been in use since the Cold War and drops his ID card into the payment acceptor. He then chooses a Coke, Diet Coke, and lemonade as his options which allows the door to open. As Dunn walks in he takes out his gun, as a cautionary measure, but puts it back after seeing he is alone. He walks straight over to the table in the center and then starts humming the lyrics to the American national anthem. The wall moves to reveal a little bookcase which houses big government containing the biggest cover-up in United States History. Drumroll please! How the government has been responsible for… wait for it! Economic failures and how it pawned off the blame on Wall Street. For starters this room in Langley does not exist. But there is definite truth to what is hidden in the imaginary box and has been going on since the inception of the U.S. in 1787. The first big "depression" came in 1837 and is uncreatively known as Panic of 1837. The panic of 1837 was ironically built off the housing bubble. Many believe that the panic was caused by banks over inflation of paper money. Yet in all honesty the collapse was due to Andrew Jackson's specie circular which meant a decrease in paper money and thus gold and silver were used as currency which led to a Gold Standard. Also this was due to the veto of the rechartering of the 2nd bank of the U.S. which caused government. money to be placed elsewhere. So even from the start it hasn't been Wall Street it has been the government that has been screwing everyone over. The next big panic occurred in 1873 (Money apparently doesn't like the numbers 7 and 3) in which was caused by worldwide financial failures due to inflation of gold by German Iron Chancellor, Otto Von Bismarck. The biggest bank failure came when Jay Cooke & Co. due to inability to sell their bonds in order to build the 2nd transcontinental railroad declared bankruptcy. This was due to U.S. Grant's monetary policy which called for raising interest rates preventing the bonds from being sold properly. Essentially what happened was that more business was occurring but the finances were reducing. So once again the government had screwed everyone and the lower classes were paying the price with unemployment rising to 14%. Then in 1929 the Great Depression hit the world caused by the stock market collapse on Black Tuesday. This however was at the time believed to be due to poor bank oversight into the market, yet in retrospect it was actually due to the Federal Reserve reducing money supply and instead made the collapse of the stock market a symptom. Also the government then enacted the Hawley-Smoot Tariff which raised the tariff on 20000 products to record highs. Once again in the biggest depression of all time it is the wonderful government who fails to lead and blames Wall Street. In what is called the worst financial crisis since the Great Depression, and is still going on today. Enter the 2008 financial crisis A.K.A. Blame Wall Street Anyway, this all started in 2006 when the housing bubble blew up and the government wanted to help the homeowners out. Then homeowners thinking that they could afford a 300K house when they made only 85K took these loans from the banks and bought these houses. However they realized, "Hey wait I can't pay the bank back."

So the bank foreclosed on these people giving them sufficient time and warning. On that topic I want to address the people complaining that they were not given sufficient notice and all that BS. Yes you were and if you were smart in the first place you wouldn't have taken a loan you knew you couldn't pay back. This is honestly just people blaming someone in order to cover for their stupidity. Then these banks were left with dead assets and billions of dollars of debt. That caused them to go bankrupt and then caused a global financial meltdown. Here once again to some extent it is the government's fault but it is also the fault of the middle class who don't understand math to realize that if you make 50 g a year you can't afford a 300k house.

On a different note the policymakers in Washington are now calling for more regulation of Wall Street through the Dodd-Frank in order to prevent another global meltdown and at the same time trying to cover their asses. Because once again it's the government's fault we are in this mess. Anyway regulation of Wall Street is beyond dumb for a bunch of reasons.

- The government doesn't know where to draw the line on regulating

Eventually regulation of banks will go to the point that for even buying a small amount of shares traders will have to call the SEC to OK it. At this point the SEC will run a background check on the buyer in order to check for any insider trading connections, then there will be a two day wait in order for papers to process, and then only will one be able to buy and trade stocks then I may as well do it myself through a place like TD Ameritrade. WHY? Because it would be so much easier.

- Financial Stability Oversight Council

The regulation bill calls for a nine person committee chaired by the Treasury Secretary himself, to overlook markets for any future meltdown. See, that's ironic because all major meltdowns in history have been due to poor actions by the government from the Great Depression to the 2008 collapse.

- Federal Reserve Control of "Inter-Connected" banks

So according to the Dodd Frank bill if a financial institution shows grave risk to stability of the economy with a 2/3rds vote they can be ousted, to this I have 1 question. Where the hell do you get off telling Wall Street how business should be run. Also you are even more of an idiot then I thought when we have seen what has happened since 2008 the economy is still reeling from truly only one bank going defunct. Let me tell you something even if you tell one of the banks to call it quits you don't think it will affect the economy, Newsflash the Wall Street Journal will read "Economy screwed once again.!"

- Rainy day fund

Or so I like to call it, anyway this regulation placed upon Wall Street will create a system that if a financial institution is not doing well that then the government has the authority to shut them down at the expense of some of Wall Street's largest institutions. Is that even legal for someone from the government to tell someone that if someone else goes under I have to pay the price.

- Shareholder-Executive Pay Package

This little provision calls for shareholders to vote on Executive Pay, which is preposterous because

1. Despite knowing maybe a little about the firm the shareholder invested in no one truly has an idea of what the executives do, because shareholders are not there monitoring them. Albeit obviously they know what they are doing, because the firms are going in the right direction and regrouping from the 2008 loss.

2. Eventually this will become a popularity contest. Say I as a shareholder don't like this guy, because I don't know he is wearing an ugly tie and then from there that bias grows chances are I am not going to say that this guy deserves to be paid adequately for the job he performs .

3. Who are you to tell me how much I should get paid. It's crass for someone who doesn't know anything about you to tell you that I don't think you are doing a very good job and that without ever having seen you work. I think that the bonus won't be coming this year.

- The President of the Federal Bank of New York will be appointed by the president

This will lead to essentially party politics because the president of the Federal Reserve Bank of New York will become a puppet for the president and just act like a dog nipping at the heel of Wall Street.

Wall Street banks control a hefty amount of U.S. Gross Domestic Product (GDP) so instead of helping the economy some congressman want to allow banks to only hold less than 10 percent of total deposit and a liability of 2% of GDP. I have a problem with this

- Once again the argument of legality comes into question. So basically the government is telling Wall Street we are going

to prevent you from controlling anything, which means
bye-bye number one economy

Earth to government -- this country fought for its independence, Ben
Franklin & Co. knew when they were signing the Declaration of
Independence. They knew they were also signing their death sentences if
the war was lost. However, they also knew that they were fighting with
people and for people. And if they lost they knew to accept the blame. So
some 300 plus years later why can't you face the fact that 2008 was your
fault and accept the consequences. Right now nobody cares about it; they
just want to get back to the lives they used to have back in 05 when life was
great. Seriously if you had any balls whatsoever you would lay off Wall
Street When all they were trying to do was help and accept responsibility. If
anything Wall Street has taken it like a man, because not once have they
retaliated despite knowing the fact that about maybe 500,000 of their
brethren are now roaming the world looking for a job. That's why Wall
Street is fed up and angry at the government. Instead of taking the blame,
they have instead decided to dig them into a deeper trench with absurd
regulations. So other people can claim that the government. is doing
something to stop the "monster" and create even more misguided hate by
the people who run the US Economy.

My parents always taught me to be respectful. Respect has helped
civilization grow otherwise we could be living in a Geico commercial where
the slogan would not be, "So easy even a caveman can do it." Now people's
respect will come if the government starts to respect them; it's happened
many a time before. That's the point of a leader: they are to lead. It's quite
easy to show respect, you see it every day from holding the door open for
other people and saying please and thank you. Sure, you might have an
ulterior motive but the gist is still the same.

See, the main problem is the voters- mainly middle class- notice that the
government shows no respect to Wall Street thus they become the enemy.
It has happened many a time with the Cubans and Russians, the
government calls them communist and we go develop bombs and drop
everything and go to war. The point of government has changed over the
years. Back in the days of George Washington it was about building a new
country that was united, in the days of Teddy Roosevelt it became about
building America as a superpower, and in the days of people like Harry Reid

and Nancy Pelosi, it's about staying in control. People mess up, and the government is run by people, but in order to cover up their mistakes the government has started blaming Wall Street. The naiveté has grown into someone on television saying "Wall Street" you get the wolves howling, bats flying through graveyard depicting the darkness that it holds. Something straight out of the opening theme to the Addams Family. If respect is shown, everyone can move on properly. (Though I do know this is quite naive)

It's a little weird when Wall Street is on your speed dial. It's also a little weird when some secretary tells his/her boss that House Democrats are on the other line. I can go on and on, but my point is that by calling every day you are only showing an inability to act and showing that you are a two faced bastard. By this I mean that it looks a little suspicious when the government calls Wall Street asking for advice showing that perhaps the people in charge don't have any idea what they are doing. Though throughout the Bush administration the financial system has been stable except for the crash but that was caused by the Clinton Administration. Though asking Wall Street shows that you have some respect, but then you go and mock them publicly with "Wall Street will pay" and stuff like that, remember Wall Street owns the world. As leaders you should:

- Accept the fact that you screwed up

This point is going to be a little harder to cleanly come out with, but if the public knows you screwed up, then Wall Street would be able to

1. Worry about fixing the economy instead of doing damage control

2. Not by still taking a bad rep and even possibly plotting revenge because let's face it nobody likes getting stiffed.

When you were a kid you had a bunch of rules, now you're all adults and generally the law is there to prevent any physical harm upon another human being. Wall Street is not a child; they are extremely good at what they do as they have shown since their inception. If anything these regulations are insulting which is basically telling Wall Street yeah we need you but we think you're out of control.

- Stop lying to the people

When the government lies, the people usually eat it up and then Wall Street starts getting blamed for everything. Seriously stop it, or if you are going to lie do it more discreetly instead of saying it was Wall Street's fault, use some other words that force the blame upon some economic phenomenon that the majority of people wouldn't understand.

- Leave the economics to Wall Street.

You went to law school, not business school; let the people with the degrees handle it. The thing many people fail to realize because they think Wall Street is out to screw them. Not true as I have proved previously. When a problem with the economy comes aboard, let Wall Street handle it, it's insulting when you don't let the experts take care of the things they spent six years and 300K plus to get. Ever notice how the economy has rebounded since it took a huge fall in 2008. Why? Thanks to the leadership of Wall Street

As you have undoubtedly noticed in the last year the US credit was downgraded and took a hit for the ages. America sees how the government has been so negligent in its duties to notice the impending doom that would be caused by this, which goes to show you that once again in a matter Wall Street had no direct control of whatsoever the government failed. America, I would now be wary of anything the government says or does.

CONCLUSION

Hopefully with this book and my constant defaming of everything you stood for, I taught you something. We need to RESPECT Wall Street, because we really truly need them. Whether you like it or not.

CITATIONS

"Bloomberg." - *Bloomberg.* N.p., n.d. Web..

"Careers for Experienced Professionals." *Careers for Experienced Professionals.*

    N.p., n.d. Web.

    <http://careers.jpmorgan.com/experienced/jpmorgan/jobs>.

"Economy of New York City." *Wikipedia.* Wikimedia Foundation, 15 Jan.

    2013. Web.

Forbes. Forbes Magazine, n.d. Web.

Fruhlinger, Josh. "Wall Street Assholes Will Eat Your Cushy Middle-Class

    Job." *Wonkette RSS.* N.p., n.d. Web.

"Goldman Sachs." *Goldman Sachs.* N.p., n.d. Web.

"History of Wall Street." *History of Wall Street.* N.p., n.d. Web.

IMDb. IMDb.com, n.d. Web.

Michael, Lewis. "- Bloomberg." - *Bloomberg.* N.p., n.d. Web.

    <http://www.bloomberg.com/apps/news?pid=newsarchive>.

"Wall Street & Stock Market History." *History of Wall Street and the Stock*

    Markets. N.p., n.d. Web.

"Wall Street." *Wikipedia*. Wikimedia Foundation, 19 Jan. 2013. Web.

ASHWIN KRISHNA KUMAR

Ashwin Krishna Kumar is a high school student in Cincinnati, Ohio. His interests include watching movies and playing basketball. He lives with his parents and two German Shepherds.

www.ingramcontent.com/pod-product-compliance
Lightning Source LLC
Chambersburg PA
CBHW030733180526
45157CB00008BA/3153

* 9 7 8 1 4 8 0 2 0 3 7 9 2 *